Forty [

God In Action

By Dion Todd

www.diontodd.org

Acknowledgments

First, I thank the Lord Jesus Christ for allowing me to write. It is something I never would have imagined myself doing during my early days. This work is certainly an example of the Lord using one of "the least of the least."

I would like to thank my dear wife, Sylvia, who has been by my side every step of the way while writing this book. Always behind the scenes proofreading and bringing me coffee, I could have never done this work without her encouragement. They say some people bring out the best in you. She inspires me to be a better man.

Thanks to the readers of our daily devotional who encouraged me to keep going, pointed out my screw ups and gave me grammar lessons along the way. It has been a walk in faith for me and we have built some great friendships.

Table of Contents

Introduction

The devotional: This book is a forty day devotional for the working class, written by one of your peers. I hope to inspire, encourage you, and give you the hope to be strong one more day through a scripture and an accompanying short story that demonstrates God in action. It is my goal to light the fire of hope within you once again.

Each entry in this book came out of prayer, praise, and worship. To get myself inspired, I go into my prayer room and shut the door. Alone with the Lord, I pray and worship at my keyboard until the Lord's presence shows up and a teaching comes. The Holy Spirit drops a subject into my mind and I simply write it down. Readers often find the words timely and relevant to their day.

Who am I: My name is Dion Todd. I grew up as an American heathen on a farm in beautiful coastal South Carolina. Hunting, fishing, off roading, dirt bikes, racing and cropping tobacco were a lot of my childhood pastimes. While growing up we rarely went to church, but we were in the heart of the Bible Belt. My Dad always taught us that there was an Almighty God, and that one day we would have to stand in front of Him and answer for the things that we had done. That saying always stuck with me, and I knew one day that I would have to meet Him, like it or not. How that happened though, was much different than I expected. I did not know that He was chasing me.

In my late teens I started playing music with local bands and lived a pretty average life as a musician until one night the Holy Spirit showed up, in the bar. I know this sounds strange, but in a flash, I suddenly knew what I wanted to do, and I was ready to get started. I put my bass in the case, told the band good night, went home, prayed and gave my life to the Lord. The next morning which was Sunday, I went to church.

Like many, I developed a very legalistic view, wanted to earn my salvation and prove my dedication to the Lord. It became a competition. I fasted for weeks, gave all that I had, tried to memorize the Bible, prayed all day, listened to the Bible all night, and made all my friends into enemies.

Believe it or not, you can do all of that and still not be very close to God, though it is all good in moderation. I knew a lot about Him, I just did not know Him. Just as Jesus said there would be those that called Him Lord Lord and He said "I never knew you", so was I. When I started to just involve God in my life every day, relax, and just include Him in whatever decision I had to make, a relationship began to develop.

Eventually I was baptized in the Holy Spirit and the Lord soon revealed to me that I had a calling into the ministry. So I enrolled in Bible college, got my Bachelor of Arts, and then became a shining vessel completely full of religion and legalism just as I thought He wanted. I had it all figured out and, man, was I smart. The chosen one had arrived. And then I...waited...

I waited twenty-five years for that door to open in ministry. During this time I was non-denominational, then a Southern Baptist, later a Pentecostal, even later a Charismatic, and then back where I started: non-denominational. I served the Lord as a painter, a carpenter, a mechanic, a musician, I.T. Tech and a computer programmer, almost anything and anywhere, except the ministry that He had mentioned. I went through a divorce, lost loved ones, had my business burn to the ground during an insurance lapse, and at one point started life over with nothing. Then I met the love of my life, remarried, and experienced many other life changing moments. It turns out that I did not know, or believe, a fraction of what I thought I did.

After decades of waiting, my shiny vessel full of religion slowly drained away, until I felt completely emptied. Where I had originally thought I knew a lot about the Bible, I now felt like I knew hardly anything. My shiny vessel full of religion was now a dusty vessel filled with the experience of life. My shallow head knowledge was replaced with a deeper heart knowledge. My legalism and looking down on others was replaced with compassion and the understanding that their sin is just like mine, bad and hard to keep behind you.

After I had finally given up on ever being in the ministry, the door finally did open and I became a creative arts pastor, which is my current day job. I was forced into it. Our computer business dried up, all jobs were closed off, and when we were packing to move out of our home this path opened to me. Like cattle herded into a trailer, I was driven into the ministry.

I truly understand how Moses set out in his youth to deliver Israel in his own strength, failed, and instead served as a shepherd for forty years in the wilderness. Then when the Lord appeared to him in the burning bush, he could only say: "Send someone else…". Moses no longer even wanted to go, but God would not take no for an answer.

Most of my life I have walked with the Lord, sometimes falling but so far managing to get back up. God has proven Himself to be faithful over the years and I have had to go back and unlearn a lot of the things that I grew up with. I have learned that for me, it is all about relationship, and not religious practices. I can be just as close to God while fishing as I can in church, even though I love attending. If you remove the personal relationship from Christianity, I want nothing to do with it. I would rather be fishing.

My style of writing: Jesus said that He would make us "fishers of men", not their hunters. When fishing, you use a lure and try to get the fish to bite. The lure has to look real and good, or the fish will run from it. The fish also has to come to you. It is not like hunting where you chase them down. Likewise, I try and make Jesus look good.

Trying to make the world live like a Christian when they do not even know Him is missing the entire point of the gospel. In my opinion, if I bring people to Jesus He will change what is wrong with them when the time is right. It is not my place to try and correct sin in people's lives; the Lord can do that when He is ready. It is my goal to bring people into a personal relationship with the Lord Jesus, and as they come to know Him, their life will fall into place.

Thank you for reading,

Dion

Bible Fun Fact: You could hire a professional mourner (Jer 9:17-18).

Day 1

† Pretty Woman †

But Rahab the prostitute and her father's household and all who belonged to her, Joshua saved alive. And she has lived in Israel to this day, because she hid the messengers whom Joshua sent to spy out Jericho. **Joshua 6:25 ESV**

The least of the least, Rahab was always looked down on by the other women of the city. She was a prostitute, covered in shame with no hope, and no future. She exchanged sex for food to simply keep her and her family alive. When she trusted in the Lord and hid the spies that Joshua sent, she was brought into the Lord's family and became the great, great grandmother of King David. She is also listed in the lineage of Jesus Christ (Matt 1:15).

One of the most anointed women that I ever saw preach was a former prostitute. Almost from the time she started speaking, demons started screaming and coming out of people in the church. She said that when she first gave her life to Christ and was delivered of crack and many other things, no normal Christians would help her. Instead, she converted some of her street walking friends and started a ministry. Now God is powerfully using them to deliver people from very bad things.

No matter what you have done, no matter where you are, God has a place for you in His family. You have not wrecked your life and it can be redeemed. There is still hope. It is not too late. He will take you and use your life to reach others that are where you used to be. Start today by praying for Him to make what is important to Him, important to you.

Prayer: *Heavenly Father, use me today. Forgive me of my past, cleanse me from all unrighteousness and help me live my life to the fullest. Make what is important to You, important to me, in the name of Jesus.*

Bible Fun Fact: *Green is the first color mentioned in the Bible (Gen 1:30).*

Day 2

† As Scary As Hell †

He ordered the furnace heated seven times more than it was usually heated. And he ordered some of the mighty men of his army to bind Shadrach, Meshach, and Abednego, and to cast them into the burning fiery furnace. ***Daniel 3:19–20 ESV***

As they were pushed to the edge of the roaring furnace, the heat coming up from the inferno killed the soldiers around them. Then they themselves were falling through the burning air, down into the fire below them. This was all because they had taken a stand for the Lord and refused to bow to Nebuchadnezzar's golden image.

I am sure it was scary as they looked down into the furnace, but they landed safely at the bottom and found they were not alone. There was a fourth Person in the furnace with them. The ropes that bound them burned off of them but they were unharmed and did not even smell like smoke. A nice touch.

You are going to make it. Though it looks as scary as hell itself, you are going to make it. Do not waver in your faith and do not compromise. When you get to the bottom you will find that you are not alone and only the things that are holding you back will be burned away.

Prayer: *Heavenly Father, I know that you are with me and that no weapon formed against me will prosper. I submit to Your will for my life and I know that you will bring me through this, in the name of Jesus.*

Bible Fun Fact: *The word "Christian" only appears three times in the Bible (Acts 11:26, 26:28, 1 Peter 4:16).*

Day 3

† Dare To Dream †

When they had crossed, Elijah said to Elisha, Ask what I shall do for you, before I am taken from you. And Elisha said, Please let there be a double portion of your spirit on me. ***2 Kings 2:9 ESV***

Walking together down the road, Elisha was just a servant. The mighty prophet Elijah was renowned for calling fire down from heaven multiple times. He caused a draught on the land, and then caused it to rain. He resurrected people from the dead, fed people for years from a small jar, and much more. He was a force to be reckoned with.

Elisha could only dream of being used by God like that. Still he asked for a double portion anointing, and the Lord gave it to him. Elijah did fourteen miracles, Elisha did twenty-eight. Exactly twice as many.

Do not be afraid to dream big. God can easily surpass your wildest dreams and go beyond your imagination, if you will go with Him. Of course, keep God centered and be a good servant / steward along the way just as Elisha did. Dare to follow your dream. It just may be that the Lord placed that within you for such a time as this.

Prayer: *Heavenly Father, give me a fresh vision and renew the dream that you gave me. I want all that You have for me Lord, in the name of Jesus.*

Bible Fun Fact: Amen means basically "so be it."

Day 4

† Going Down For The Last Time †

My sheep hear My voice, and I know them, and they follow Me. I give them eternal life, and they will never perish, and no one will snatch them out of My hand. My Father, who has given them to Me, is greater than all, and no one is able to snatch them out of the Father's hand. **John 10:26–29 ESV**

The star of the show that we were watching took some really bad knocks and it looked like he was going down for the last time. Somehow he found some inner strength and soon pulled himself together, got back up and gave the bad guy what was coming to him. The hero always gets back up after a knock down.

Life can be full of setbacks, disappointments and failures but the God we serve is stronger than all and no one is able to snatch us from Him. God is stronger than any addiction, demon, person, task or circumstance that you face today.

The only thing that truly matters is your relationship with Him. When you are in His hand nothing is going to touch you without Him allowing it for some purpose. I am not saying that you will never be sick or in need. I am saying that you will never be alone, and you will never be lost because our God is able to sustain you.

He is able to make all things work out for your good. Even the things that were meant to harm you will instead promote you. You will not go down for the last time because God will always give you the strength to get back up.

Prayer: *Heavenly Father, I pray that you give me the grace to always get up when I fall. Help me see things the way that You do and draw my heart to You, in the name of Jesus.*

Bible Fun Fact: The first musical instrument mentioned in the bible is the Harp: (Gen 4:21).

Day 6

† The Lord is My Rock †

He said, The LORD is my rock and my fortress and my deliverer, my God, my rock, in whom I take refuge, my shield, and the horn of my salvation, my stronghold and my refuge, my savior; You save me from violence. I call upon the LORD, who is worthy to be praised, and I am saved from my enemies. 2 Samuel 22:1–4 ESV

David sang this song to the Lord when he was delivered from all of his enemies. Where others saw nothing, David saw the works of the Lord through the eyes of faith. When those around him did not believe, he could truthfully say, "I call upon the Lord, who is worthy to be praised, and I am saved from my enemies. It works for me, see the dead giant head I am holding?"

He would have had nothing to sing about at all if he had not lived through some pretty hard times. You do not get the glory without the story. You do not have a testimony without a test. Though invisible to our normal eye, the Lord is there to help us. An unshakable Rock, the Ancient of Days, The Living God. When we invite the Lord into our situation, it changes, and when God is on our side, no one can stand against us.

Do not struggle in your own strength. Invite the Lord into your situation. Ask the Lord to come help you with this. Don't become discouraged when it takes longer than you thought. David went through many afflictions, but God delivered him out of them all.

Prayer: *Heavenly Father, please come and be a part of my life today. I look to You Lord. Save me from my enemies and give me wisdom to excel, in the name of Jesus.*

Bible Fun Fact: The middle chapter in the Bible is Psalm 117.

Day 6

† The Oak Tree †

He said therefore, What is the kingdom of God like? And to what shall I compare it? It is like a grain of mustard seed that a man took and sowed in his garden, and it grew and became a tree, and the birds of the air made nests in its branches. **Luke 13:18 ESV**

As I stared out of the window at the huge oak tree in our yard, I thought of what it looked like thirty years ago, when I first moved here. It was a small scrawny thing then. Now it is a huge tree and you could park several cars in it's shade. It has limbs bigger than my torso.

It did not happen overnight. This magnificent oak took decades to get where it is now, and it could have easily been crushed or uprooted while it was still small. There was a time when it was small and weak but over time, using what God has provided for it each day, it has now become a mature oak tree.

The faith that is in you starts small, but it grows over time. As you walk with the Lord, talk with the Lord, and rely on His provision, that little seed within you will grow and become unshakable. Don't try and rush it. You will become disappointed. Take it one day at a time and some day when you look back on where you are now, you will laugh. Faith and oak trees both have to grow over time.

Prayer: *Heavenly Father, be with me this day and provide the things that I need to grow. Strengthen my faith and guide my steps with Your Holy Spirit, in the name of Jesus.*

Bible Fun Fact: *The longest verse in the Bible: Esther 8:9 (78 words).*

Day 7

† Why Question Me? †

Then Abraham fell on his face and laughed and said to himself, Shall a child be born to a man who is a hundred years old? Shall Sarah, who is ninety years old, bear a child? **Genesis 17:17 ESV**

Abraham lay on his face and laughed when God told him that he would soon have a son because he was almost one-hundred years old, and his wife Sarah was ninety. Still, the following year they had a son named Isaac. What God told Abraham had now come to pass.

God is more than able to bring to pass the things that He has told you. Though you have now waited so long for something that you wanted so badly that it makes you upset to think about it, you are closer now than ever before. In the past, I have given up on things that He told me twenty years earlier, and then watched them come to pass. He is faithful.

Do not give up on the things that God has told you. Though they tarry, wait for them. He gave you the promise to help you hold on through the difficult times like now. Stay the course and stop questioning His promise.

Prayer: *Heavenly Father, I believe that You will come through for me. Please show Yourself strong in My life. I know that You spoken the sun into existence and you can take care of me today, in the name of Jesus.*

Bible Fun Fact: There are 6,468 commands given in the Bible.

Day 8

† It Is Listening - Not The Lottery †

*And Elijah said to her, Do not fear; go and do as you have said. But first make me a little cake of it and bring it to me, and afterward make something for yourself and your son. For thus says the LORD, the God of Israel, The jar of flour shall not be spent, and the jug of oil shall not be empty, until the day that the LORD sends rain upon the earth. **1 Kings 17:13–14 ESV***

As I listened to the preacher pray over the offering basket, he prayed that all the money given would be returned one hundred fold. Another day, another offering I thought. This was nothing new to me as I had heard that speech before and given in many offerings.

This time though I heard something else. The Lord was nudging me and He wanted me to give much more than usual. At the time I probably made a couple of hundred a week and after tithing 10 percent, things were pretty tight. Still, the feeling wouldn't go away.

I had forty dollars on me and I placed that in the

offering basket. It was all that I had at the time, a bit like the widow's two mites. I left church with just enough gas to get home. The following week, someone gave me $4,000. It was not a loan and they did not go to church. They said "we felt like we should help you." God had returned my gift one hundred fold and from an unexpected outside source.

Certainly you should not be suckered in by long-winded speeches of greed, but there are times when the Lord asks you for a little, and then He will turn it into a lot. God is not a piñata and your giving is not a stick. It is your obedience to His timely prompting that counts.

Prayer: *Heavenly Father, please show me divine opportunities and make it clear when I should give. Teach me Your will Lord, in the name of Jesus.*

Bible Fun Fact: *Methuselah was the oldest man in the Bible at 969 yrs old (Gen 5:27).*

Day 9

† Suddenly †

If He comes suddenly, do not let Him find you sleeping. ***Mark 13:36 NIV***

There was a time in our life when our business started failing and our income got less, and less, and then stopped. As the bills started piling up, we tried everything, but nothing seemed to help. We gave more, prayed more, fasted more, served more, tried to find any job possible and then as the last straw, we prepared to move out of our home.

After months of this, I no longer had the energy or will power to pray anymore. One morning during the week that we were preparing to move, I went into my prayer room and just sat there, mostly contemplating how much I would miss it. The Lord spoke to me that morning, and within twenty-four hours our life had completely changed for the better. That is how I became a pastor.

God closed the old out and brought in something new. It hurt to see the old go, but the new was so much better. God moves suddenly at what we often think is the very last minute. It is not to Him. He knew the day that the transition would take place and He was right on time. Our fear and worry were for nothing.

God knows where you are and He has the day marked on His calendar when your circumstance will suddenly change. Don't give up yet. We don't know the day or the hour, but the Father does and He will not be late, nor early. The change will come suddenly.

Prayer: *Heavenly Father, I pray that you meet my needs and move in my life. Draw me into a deeper relationship with You and give me a fresh zeal today, in the name of Jesus.*

Bible Fun Fact: Assuming your Bible is 1000 pages long, and you read a page every 5 minutes, it should take you 84 hours or just under 3 and a half days to read it all.

Day 10

† Silence In The Classroom †

He succeeded in everything he undertook. But when envoys were sent by the rulers of Babylon to ask him about the miraculous sign that had occurred in the land, God left him to test him and to know everything that was in his heart. **2 Chronicles 32:30–31 NIV**

Hezekiah was a great king in Judah who followed the Lord closely. At his prayer, God sent an angel and wiped out 185,000 Assyrians who were coming to attack Jerusalem (2 Kings 19:35). At his prayer, God healed him and added fifteen years to his life (2 Kings 20:6). Still, there was a time when God left him to test him and to know what was in his heart.

When a teacher is teaching the class, you can ask all the relevant questions that you have about the subject and the teacher will answer them. However when the test comes, there is silence in the classroom.

I know scripture says that He will never leave nor

forsake you, but there is a difference in the omnipresence of God which is everywhere and His manifest presence which may or may not be in the room with you.

Those are the times when there is no answer and your tears seem to go unnoticed. When you feel that God has gotten you out on a limb and then abandoned you. Know that you are not really alone. You are simply entering the test phase of what you have been learning. You continue on with the last word given until you have a new one. There is always silence in the classroom during a test.

Prayer: *Heavenly Father, I pray that You strengthen me and give me the grace to get through these times. Please reveal the pride in my life to me so that I can deal with it before it harms me, in the name of Jesus.*

Bible Fun Fact: *Ehud was the first left-handed man in the Bible (Judges 3:15).*

Day 11

† Prospering Under Pagans †

And Pharaoh said to his servants, Can we find a man like this, in whom is the Spirit of God? Then Pharaoh said to Joseph, Since God has shown you all this, there is none so discerning and wise as you are. You shall be over my house, and all my people shall order themselves as you command. **Genesis 41:37–40 ESV**

While serving a prison sentence after he was falsely accused of attempted rape, Joseph was summoned to appear before Pharaoh. Though he was innocent, he had now spent years in prison and it appeared that he would be executed. I am sure all of these thoughts passed through his mind. "Why else would Pharaoh summon me? They certainly hanged that baker…"

After shaving and changing his clothes, Joseph was brought in before Pharaoh. He probably breathed a sigh of relief when Pharaoh said "I have had a dream and there is no one who can interpret it".

Joseph was used by God to interpret the dream and was then made the one in charge of Egypt. Daniel was used by God and made the one in charge of Babylon (Daniel 2:48). Mordecai was used by God and made the one in charge of Persia (Esther 10:3). Esther became a queen (Esther 2:17).

All of these people who were slaves, prisoners and exiles were living in a pagan nation that served other gods and idols, yet they prospered because they served God Almighty. God is able to make you shine above the rest. He is able to protect and prosper you no matter what laws they pass. God can make you prosper while under pagans.

Prayer: *Heavenly Father, work Your will in my life today. Teach me to hear Your voice and give me the grace to carry it out, in the name of Jesus.*

Bible Fun Fact: *There was a lady named Noah (Josh 17:3).*

Day 12

† The Stress Test †

Therefore, since we are surrounded by so great a cloud of witnesses, let us also lay aside every weight, and sin which clings so closely, and let us run with endurance the race that is set before us, looking to Jesus, the founder and perfecter of our faith, who for the joy that was set before Him endured the cross, despising the shame, and is seated at the right hand of the throne of God.
Hebrews 12:1–2 ESV

As the treadmill stepped up to another difficulty level, it became more and more difficult to keep up with it. Every three minutes it increased the incline and speed until I was literally running uphill. I had monitors taped all over me and the hospital staff was closely watching a computer screen with little jagged lines that scrolled by while it recorded my progress.

Before I started, I had asked them if there was a time limit or a difficulty goal and they said just run until you cannot run anymore. When I asked about a level cap, they just smiled and said no one beats the machine. After four or five increases, I totally agreed and finally told them that I could not go on. At that point it was more like torture than a stress test. They began to slow the treadmill where I could get off but that took a little while. (For those wondering, they said I did excellent).

When walking with God there are times when we will endure a stress test. Jesus Himself did because it was written that he endured the cross and His sweat was as great drops of blood (Luke 22:44). During these times, there is a great cloud of witnesses watching us take this test and no matter how much faith you have, God has a test for that level. At a point in my life, I thought that I had great faith but God had a great test for it. In the end, I was a broken man. No one beats the machine because it scales accordingly. If you disagree, read the book of Job again and picture yourself in his place.

God knows how much you can take and He is not out to kill you. When you have finally reached your limit He will slow the treadmill. Like me though, you may find that you can go much further than you thought you could and you will be stronger in the end.

Prayer: *Heavenly Father, give me grace and strength to serve you with all of my heart. Help me face the challenges that come with the right attitude, in the name of Jesus I pray.*

Bible Fun Fact: Noah's Ark was 450' long, 75' wide, and 45' high, and had 3 stories (Gen 6:15-16).

Day 13

† The Poppin' John †

For land that has drunk the rain that often falls on it, and produces a crop useful to those for whose sake it is cultivated, receives a blessing from God. But if it bears thorns and thistles, it is worthless and near to being cursed, and its end is to be burned. **Hebrews 6:7–8 ESV**

Each spring when we got ready to plant the garden, Dad would break out the old 1940s John Deere tractor we owned. We called it the Poppin' John because of the way that it sputtered and backfired. Even then it was about 35 years old. He would plow the field and the kids would walk behind and pull out the roots, rocks and anything else that did not belong there. After the field was prepared, we were able to plant and we always had a great garden. We worked together and it took actual work to make it happen.

God is after fruit in your life. He digs deep and brings things to the surface that we like to keep hidden in secret. At that point, we have to deal with it and He will then give you the grace to do so. The weeds and rocks have to be removed from your life or they will choke out what He is trying to grow. The anger, the bitterness and oh so much more that we will not mention in public.

Don't go on a witch hunt and try and find areas that He has not revealed yet. If you get in front of the tractor you may get run over. Just work with Him and as He reveals things, repent and deal with them one at a time. The work is not easy and most will not do it. This process repeats just like planting the garden year after year. He reveals things, you agree and work with Him without trying to hide it. It is then removed from your life. God will bring forth the fruit of the spirit in your life as you walk with Him, one day at a time.

Prayer: *Heavenly Father, reveal the things in my life that need to be dealt with and give me the grace to handle it. Prepare me Lord and take away the weeds, in the name of Jesus I pray.*

__Bible Fun Fact:__ Moses changed Hoshea's name to Joshua (Num 13:16).

Day 14

† Rock Bottom †

And the LORD appointed a great fish to swallow up Jonah. And Jonah was in the belly of the fish three days and three nights. Then Jonah prayed to the LORD his God from the belly of the fish, saying, I called out to the LORD, out of my distress, and he answered me __Jonah 1:16–2:2 ESV__

Sitting in the black darkness all alone, Jonah contemplated his situation from the inside of a great fish. The Lord had told him to go preach, but Jonah decided to do something else entirely, and went the other way. In time, his past caught up with him and swallowed him alive. Now it looked like the end. He had disobeyed, and this was his punishment. He deserved it, it is over, 'bout as well lay down and die.

Then some spark of hope arose in Jonah, as his life was fainting away (2:7) he prayed to the Lord and God changed his circumstances. God spoke to the fish and it took Jonah back to the land and spit him out. Peter thought that he had wrecked his life as well when he denied even knowing the Lord Jesus three times in one night (Mark 14:72), but the Lord restored him.

I am not saying that sin and running away from God is alright. I am saying that with a simple prayer, you can make it right. Sometimes when we run from God, He will allow us to hit rock bottom. Then when we turn to Him, He will help us. It is never too late, because God's love has no limits. It is never too late, because when you hit rock bottom, He can restore you just as He did Jonah, Peter and me.

Prayer: *Heavenly Father, pick me up when I fall. Blow your breath on the fire within me and cause me to stand firm on Your word, in the name of Jesus I pray.*

Bible Fun Fact: *There are 12 books of the Bible that start with J.*

Day 15

† I See Nothing There †

And Peter answered Him, Lord, if it is You, command me to come to You on the water. He said, Come. So Peter got out of the boat and walked on the water and came to Jesus. **Matthew 14:28–29 ESV**

Waves splashed against the side of the boat and the light of the moon shone across the water as Peter and the other disciples stared at Jesus, thinking that He was a ghost. When Jesus told Peter to come, Peter stood in the boat and looked at the water, but there was nothing there to be seen, except for the water, and Jesus standing on it.

All of his common sense and experience as a fisherman told him if you step out there, you will drown. The rest of the disciples knew it as well. Everyone knew better than to try to walk on water. Peter pushed these thoughts out of his mind and took a tentative step. Before his foot touched the water, it became solid and supported him. Though he could see nothing there, when he stepped out in faith, there was something there to catch him.

That is living faith, obeying even though it looks impossible. Matters of faith are rarely understood by the mind. Once you say "I cannot do that", you have prophesied your own future. All the heroes of the Bible spoke positively and in faith. Joshua commanded the sun to stand still (Joshua 10:12) and it did. Elijah commanded it not to rain and it did not for three and a half years (James 5:17).

We are to work together with God to accomplish His will on the earth. He may ask us to do things that we do not have the means to do. At that point, He will provide whatever is needed, though we may see nothing there. It will be there right before your foot hits the water.

Prayer: *Heavenly Father, help me see the unseen. Help me believe and build my faith, in the name of Jesus I pray.*

Day 16

† Home Is On The Other Side †

Fear not, for I have redeemed you; I have called you by name, you are mine. When you pass through the waters, I will be with you; and through the rivers, they shall not overwhelm you; when you walk through fire you shall not be burned, and the flame shall not consume you. **Isaiah 43:1–2 ESV**

It was almost dark and we had to ride our motorcycles through the swamp to get back home. We had done it many times, but this time it had rained a lot and we came to a place where the trail was completely flooded out. Home was on the other side and we had to go through the water to get there. I started in and could see the red sandy bottom of the stream as I started through the water. Then I saw the water turn dark and the front wheel dipped down.

Thinking it was just a dip and that it would surely come up the other side, I hit the gas. The next thing I knew I was swimming in fast running water with limbs and debris streaming past me. It was shoulder deep. The motorcycle was laying on the bottom of the creek. It was scary. I had to fish around on the bottom to find the motorcycle and drag it out. We removed the spark plug, drained the water from it and pushed for about half a mile before we got it started again, then we made it on home.

It is always scary to face a trial, but God will bring you through it and you will make it to the other side. There is no testimony without passing through the test. There is no glory without first living the story. There is no victory without a challenge. In this scripture, they went through the water, but God got them through to the other side.

No matter what you are going through today, God wants you to overcome but you will have to put on your gloves and fight if you want it. He wants you to be a winner, and if you will simply walk with Him one day at a time you will beat this thing. Home is on the other side.

Prayer: *Heavenly Father, I pray that you help me pass through whatever trial I may face. I trust in You and know that you have my best interest in mind, in the name of Jesus.*

Bible Fun Fact: Three of the four women at the crucifixion were named Mary (Jn 19:25).

Day 17

† Three Hundred †

And the LORD said to Gideon, "With the 300 men who lapped I will save you and give the Midianites into your hand, and let all the others go every man to his home." So the people took provisions in their hands, and their trumpets. And he sent all the rest of Israel every man to his tent, but retained the 300 men. Judges 7:7–8 ESV

Gideon had begun his journey with over 32,000 men. Now he stood with only three hundred facing an enemy army of over 135,000. He was afraid, but followed God one command at a time. It was a crazy plan; they were going to sneak up on a giant enemy army while they were sleeping, then use trumpets and hidden torches to surprise them, but then what…

It worked. When they blew the trumpets and smashed the jars to reveal the torches, the enemy panicked and started killing each other. Before long, they ran from the battlefield, broken and defeated. Gideon and the men of Israel pursued them and completely defeated Midian and their kings. From this victory, the land had rest for forty years.

When God is on your side, it is not what you have or how much of it that will determine your outcome. When Gideon awoke the giant sleeping army, they could have easily turned and killed him. It was God that fought the battle and He gave Gideon the victory. You only have to follow one step at a time to win this battle. Don't stop, don't turn back, keep putting one foot in front of the other one and you will come out a winner.

Prayer: *Heavenly Father, be my guide today. Help me to hear Your voice like Gideon did and give me the grace to obey it, in the name of Jesus.*

Bible Fun Fact: *Daniel prayed on his knees three times a day (Dan 6:10).*

Day 18

† The End Of The Line †

Why is the LORD bringing us into this land, to fall by the sword? Our wives and our little ones will become a prey. Would it not be better for us to go back to Egypt? And they said to one another, "Let us choose a leader and go back to Egypt."
Numbers 14:2–4 ESV

The Israelites were standing on the border of the land that God had promised to give them. God had done incredible signs and wonders in their lives and had just delivered them from slavery in Egypt. Now, when so close to a major breakthrough, they stubbornly refused to take the next step. They wanted to kill Moses, appoint a new leader and return to Egypt. They would do anything except what God asked them to do, and they had now reached the end of the line. They would go no further.

I have seen many people get stalled in life because they could not take that next step. While standing on the border of their own promised land, they were too terrified or stubborn to do what God asked, and they just sat there. Some of us should have left that place fifteen years ago, but we could not let it go. There are pastors in churches that should have left years ago, but they they still sit there fossilized. God will not make you obey. He will let you die off and use your children when you refuse to take the next step.

You can break the cycle. Choose to obey the Lord's prompting, it is for your own good. Though it looks short term scary, it will be long term beneficial. Pray hard and take the risk. If you feel that you have been left behind and are no longer where you should be, repent, get up and take the next step. God will restore you and put you back on track.

Prayer: *Heavenly Father, give me the grace to follow you wherever you call me. Help me to face any obstacle and stay in step with You. Let me be the one that enters the land and does not retreat, in the name of Jesus.*

Bible Fun Fact: *Saul was so afraid when they tried to make him king that he hid in some luggage so they couldn't find him (1 Sam 10:22).*

Day 19

† Relax †

Humble yourselves, therefore, under the mighty hand of God so that at the proper time He may exalt you, casting all your anxieties on Him, because He cares for you. ***1 Peter 5:6–7 ESV***

Laying in bed and unable to sleep, another night passed by. So concerned about the next day, that I could not seem to end the current one. Yet when the following day arrived, everything took care of itself. Day after day, year after year, decade after decade, the pattern continues. Worry is for nothing, anxiety accomplishes nothing, and when the problem arrives, so does God's provision.

Stop striving to make something happen too soon, or in your own strength. When the time comes, it will be unstoppable and so easy that you will say, "How can it be?". I have worked at things so hard in my life that I became frustrated and gave up, then watched it come to pass without having to lifting a finger to help. Even my "giving up" did not stop God's promises from coming to pass in my life. It is He who is faithful, not me.

Relax, stop striving, stop worrying and being so anxious about the future. Submit yourself to God, put Him first, delight in the Lord and all of these things will take care of themselves in the proper time. He cares for you and He gave you the dream that you carry inside. Relax, take it one step at a time. Love Him and let Him bring it to pass.

Prayer: *Heavenly Father, I wait on You. I know that you have not forgotten me and I trust that You will take care of me, in the name of Jesus I pray.*

Bible Fun Fact: *A man who was a newlywed was exempt from military service for a year (Deut 24:5).*

Day 20

† Seventy-Two Hours †

And when David and his men came to the city, they found it burned with fire, and their wives and sons and daughters taken captive. Then David and the people who were with him raised their voices and wept until they had no more strength to weep. **1 Samuel 30:2–4 ESV**

David stood amidst the burned ashes of his city with tears running down his face. Though he was anointed as king years ago, he had been running from Saul ever since. Now while the men were away, Amalekites had burned the city and carried off all of their wives and children. His own men were talking of stoning him to death. This was a difficult time for David. One that would break most men, but he strengthened himself in God (1 Sam 30:6).

In seventy-two hours, everything changed (2 Sam 1:2). With God's help, David rescued their families and recovered all (1 Sam 30:18). Saul died during a battle with the Philistines (1 Sam 31:3). They made David king over Judah (2 Sam 2:4). The breakthrough was so close and things that had not changed for years, were now only hours away.

David did not know this and if he had given up and fallen on his sword, he would have missed the greatest years of his life.

It is always darkest right before the breakthrough. The battle can become so intense that you want to quit, but hang on. A lot can change in seventy-two hours. You are closer than ever to seeing the promises of God fulfilled in your life.

Prayer: *Heavenly Father, give me a heart like David that will trust You even in the face of adversity. Strengthen me Lord and help me to see past the problem, in the name of Jesus I pray.*

Bible Fun Fact: *A city in Egypt was named Memphis (Hos 9:6).*

Day 21

† The Black Sheep †

Out of that terrible travail of soul, he'll see that it's worth it and be glad he did it. Through what he experienced, my righteous one, my servant, will make many "righteous ones," as he himself carries the burden of their sins. Therefore I'll reward him extravagantly— the best of everything, the highest honors—Because he looked death in the face and didn't flinch, because he embraced the company of the lowest. He took on his own shoulders the sin of the many, he took up the cause of all the black sheep. **Isaiah 53:11 ESV**

I grew up as the least of my family, who at the time was the least of another family. The youngest of thirteen kids and a stepchild on top of that. Every day, it was made clear that I did not belong there and never would.

Have you ever felt like the black sheep in the family? Made some mistakes, or maybe like me, you are the mistake and never able to get free of it? After enough pain we become closed off to the world.

Be encouraged. Jesus has friends in low places and He found me there. Jesus redeemed me, added me to His family and healed my heart. He took up the cause of troubled and hurting people and He will take your burden today if you will let Him.

Remember, today is the first day of the rest of your life. What you have been in the past is gone and you decide who you will be from this day forward. Remember that if you are a black sheep, your brightest days are still ahead of you!

Prayer: *Heavenly Father, I believe that You are there for me. When the world looks the other way, You still look my way. Help me to see the world through Your eyes, in the name of Jesus I pray.*

Bible Fun Fact: When Moses lead the people out of Egypt, he took the bones of Joseph with them. (Ex 13:19)

Day 22

† The Bumpy Road †

But Ruth said, Do not urge me to leave you or to return from following you. For where you go I will go, and where you lodge I will lodge. Your people shall be my people, and your God my God. Where you die I will die, and there will I be buried. **Ruth 1:16–17 ESV**

Ruth walked along the road thinking about what had recently happened. Her husband had died, her father-in-law had died, and her brother-in-law as well. Now it was just her and Naomi her mother-in-law, and they were penniless.

Naomi urged Ruth to turn back and go home to her family, but Ruth clung to her. Ruth told Naomi, "Where you go, I will go, and where you stay, I will stay." Even though much hardship lay before them, that is where Ruth's destiny was. God blessed Ruth after this, and she is in the lineage of Jesus.

Sometimes we find that our destiny lies down the difficult path, and while on the way we are given a choice to turn back. Many turned back from following Jesus. Stay the course. God will fulfill His promises to you just as He did with Ruth, though it can be a bumpy road along the way.

Prayer: *Heavenly Father, help me to see the path that You have for me clearly. Please give me the grace to face this time and victory over those that would harm me, in the name of Jesus I pray.*

Bible Fun Fact: The time period of the book of Genesis spans more time than all of the rest of the Bible combined.

Day 23

† The Caterpillar †

*But our citizenship is in heaven, and from it we await a Savior, the Lord Jesus Christ, who will transform our lowly body to be like His glorious body, by the power that enables Him even to subject all things to Himself. **Phil 3:20-21 ESV***

Each year, at an oak tree in our yard, a fresh batch of caterpillars are born into the world. They first crawl about as tiny helpless worms stuck in the tree. After much effort, they find a spot to call home, build a cocoon, and shut themselves off from the world. After a few weeks of being in the dark, the air is filled with butterflies.

When walking with the Lord, we all start out excited, but difficult times do come. Rarely is this Christian walk that easy to do, but it is all preparing us for something better. The word transform in this verse means to remodel. To take what is there, and make it new again. The Lord does not destroy what we are, He makes us better.

Let the Lord remodel you into something better.

Don't give up when you are alone and it gets dark, this is just part of the process. If you give up now, you will miss the most glorious part of your life. Right when the caterpillar thought it was over, it became a butterfly.

Prayer: *Heavenly Father, I choose to serve You through the dark times as well as the light. Grant me courage and grace to follow You through whatever I may face, in the name of Jesus I pray.*

Bible Fun Fact: The spies that Moses sent into Canaan returned with grapes, figs, and pomegranates (Num 13:23).

Day 24

† Your Testimony †

Beloved, do not be surprised at the fiery trial when it comes upon you to test you, as though something strange were happening to you. But rejoice insofar as you share Christ's sufferings, that you may also rejoice and be glad when his glory is revealed.
1Pet. 4:12 ESV

I have a testimony that I share sometimes where the Lord gave me a horrible job in a plant polishing brass and sweeping the floor. Within a year, I was the manager and everyone that worked there was saved. When I went to church, I filled my entire row with guests. The pastor loved me. If I had not lost my previous job I would not have this testimony.

Unless a test comes, there is no testimony. Testimony, witness, a matter of fact, are things that come from our experience. These are the things you can stand on when the going gets tough. Things that you hear from others help, but the things that you have lived are your testimony and will help you, and others.

When you look at what Jesus has already brought you through, you know that He will bring you through this as well. Just as David killed the lion, the bear and was now ready for Goliath, the Lord will turn your test into a testimony. The things that you now suffer will work out for your own good in due time.

Prayer: *Heavenly Father, I know that You are with me and will bring me through whatever I face. I pray that You have Your way in my life today and draw my heart to You, in the name of Jesus.*

Day 25

† When You Cannot Face the Wind †

Now when the south wind blew gently, supposing that they had obtained their purpose, they weighed anchor and sailed along Crete, close to the shore. But soon a tempestuous wind, called the northeaster, struck down from the land. And when the ship was caught and could not face the wind, we gave way to it and were driven along. **Acts 27:13-15 ESV**

Paul was now a prisoner and being carried by ship to eventually witness to Caesar, but on the way they were caught in a terrible storm. They could not face the strength of the wind and were driven by the storm for two weeks, completely out of control.

However, they were completely in God's control because He controlled the wind that drove them. They finally landed on a beach, and the Holy Spirit used Paul to heal all the diseases on the entire island of Malta. They all came to know the Lord. It was just a side trip on his journey.

Sometimes in life we face winds like this, and no amount of prayer, or giving, or crying seems to change our course. Just remember that when a storm blows you off course that God is controlling the direction of the wind. We will be driven right to where God wants us to be.

Prayer: *Heavenly Father, I know that You control the wind and that this will pass. I will come through this and have a testimony of Your greatness in the name of Jesus I pray.*

Bible Fun Fact: *The daughter of Jairus was twelve years old when Jesus brought her back to life (Lk 8:42).*

Day 26

† Just Around the Corner †

And they went a three days journey in the wilderness of Etham and camped at Marah. And they set out from Marah and came to Elim; at Elim there were twelve springs of water and seventy palm trees, and they camped there. **Numbers 33:8–9 ESV**

The Israelites had been traveling for three days through a desert wasteland when they arrived at Marah, thirsty and out of water. The water at Marah was bitter (poisoned) and they could not drink it so they began to grumble against Moses. When Moses prayed, God showed him a tree that he threw into the water and it became sweet.

Their very next stop was Elim, where there were twelve springs of water. An abundance of water, a spring for each of the twelve tribes and even seventy palm trees for them to rest under. More than they asked for. This test was no water in sight, but it was just around the corner. The next test was no food in sight, but it was just around the corner.

Do not give up when what you need is not yet in sight. It is just a test of your faith. You will have the chance to trust God, or to murmur and complain each time. What you need is waiting just around the next corner.

Prayer: *Heavenly Father, I know that You love me and the things that I need, You will provide for me. I choose to trust You today, in the name of Jesus I pray.*

Day 27

† The Dead End †

I will instruct you and teach you in the way you should go; I will counsel you with my loving eye on you. **Psalms 32:8 NIV**

Recently when the Lord was ready to start something new in our life, He started closing out the old. Of course we panicked, tried giving more, praying more, fasting more, serving more, but nothing helped. So we decided we would do this, but this turned out to be a dead end. Then we decided we would do that, but that went nowhere either.

It seemed that each time that we were about to give up, something would appear to give us a little hope, but then turn out to be a dead end. In time, the Lord opened the door that we were supposed to go through and it turned out great. All the worry, struggling and despair was for nothing. God had a plan that we could not see and He had to close down part one before He could begin part two.

The next time that you are looking at one dead end after another, know that God is bringing something new to your life, and it is going to be good. The chaos that is going on in your mind will be for nothing. It is just a transition to something new and better, and the dead end is part of the process.

Prayer: *Heavenly Father, please help me see past the dead end and know that You are working behind the scenes. I know that the plans that You have for me are good and the right door will open, in the name of Jesus I pray.*

Bible Fun Fact: Joab's house was located in the wilderness (1 Kg 2:33-34).

Day 28

† The Wine Press †

Oh, magnify the LORD with me, and let us exalt His name together! I sought the LORD, and He answered me and delivered me from all my fears. Those who look to Him are radiant, and their faces shall never be ashamed. This poor man cried, and the LORD heard him and saved him out of all his troubles. **Psalms 34:3–6 ESV**

David was now in the enemies' camp and surrounded by the relatives of those that he had killed in battle. Saul had intended to kill him in order to preserve his kingship and David had to get out of the country quickly. He crossed the border and entered the Philistine town of Gath hoping to hide from Saul. Gath appropriately means "the wine press". David was now out of the frying pan and into the fire.

Not long after this the people began to talk about David: "Is this not David who they sing about? Saul has struck down his thousands, and David his ten thousands?" David was under immense pressure, so much pressure that he started to act like he was mad (1Sam 21:13). They finally let him go and

David then wrote Psalm 34. This poor man cried and the Lord heard him and saved him!

The man who slew bears, lions, and Goliath was pressed like a grape until fear came to the surface. He was taken to the edge of his faith and it looked dark and hopeless, yet God delivered him. No matter how big your faith is, God is able to stretch it a bit further. His tests scale infinitely. Still, He is always there to deliver you in the end. Will you trust Him while in the wine press? It is amazing what comes out.

Prayer: *Heavenly Father, strengthen me and help me serve You today without shrinking back. Let Your love and peace cover me, in the name of Jesus I pray.*

Bible Fun Fact: Only two nuts are mentioned by name in the Bible: almonds and pistachios.

Day 29

✝ Darkest Before the Dawn ✝

*And while he was still speaking with them, the messenger came down to him and said, This trouble is from the LORD! Why should I wait for the LORD any longer? But Elisha said, Hear the word of the LORD: thus says the LORD, Tomorrow about this time... **2Kings 6:33-7:1 ESV***

Joram was king when Samaria, the capital city of Israel, was besieged by Syria about 850 BC. Samaria was surrounded and a great famine spread through out the city. People were literally eating each other. This was a very dark time for the people of Samaria and the king begin to blame God.

Finally the king snapped and decided that if he could not kill God, he would kill the man of God, and set out to find Elisha. Elisha though had a completely different view and told them that by the following day food would be so plentiful that it would cost pennies. What he said came to pass the following day.

Your breakthrough is waiting near your breaking point. When it looks like you cannot go on and it becomes dark, and you are ready to let God have it with both barrels, you are so close. Don't give up! It is always the darkest right before the dawn.

Prayer: *Heavenly Father, I ask that you strengthen me and guide me through this time. Lord, I cannot do this without You! Send Your Comforter to me today, in the name of Jesus I pray.*

Bible Fun Fact: *Malachi, written about 400 BC, is the youngest book in the Old Testament.*

Day 30

† Schooling †

As the rain and the snow come down from heaven, and do not return to it without watering the earth and making it bud and flourish, so that it yields seed for the sower and bread for the eater, so is my word that goes out from my mouth: It will not return to me empty, but will accomplish what I desire and achieve the purpose for which I sent it. **Isaiah 55:10–11 NIV**

The Lord spoke to me when I was about twenty years old and told me that I would one day be in the ministry and to prepare myself. I was very excited and entered seminary while continuing to work a day job. I graduated, and continued to work various day jobs for the next 20 years ending up in computers, programming, and technical stuff, all while waiting.

When I had given up and pretty much forgotten what the Lord had told me, I was suddenly pushed into the ministry just like cattle being herded down a chute. It required no more effort than putting one foot in front of the other, but a lot of endurance. Now I use the skills that I learned in my past for the Lord.

Even though I had graduated Bible college, I was not done with my schooling.

What the Lord has told you will come to pass, and you can build your life on it. The things that you are doing today are preparing you to be used tomorrow.

Prayer: *Heavenly Father, I know that You have a plan for my life. Please reveal it to me in a way that I understand. Help me get in tune with You and give me a clear vision, in the name of Jesus I pray.*

Bible Fun Fact: Jubal invented the harp and flute (Gen 4:21).

Day 31

† The Waterfall †

Deep calls to deep at the roar of your waterfalls; all your breakers and your waves have gone over me. **Psalms 42:7 ESV**

Moments before the water was still and quiet as they drifted down the stream. They were relaxed in the warm sunshine, not noticing the low roar coming. Suddenly, their lives flashed before their eyes and they began to panic as they realized they were quickly approaching a waterfall, and now it was too late to get off. Screaming loudly they went over the cliff, completely out of control, and splashed into a surprisingly tranquil pool below.

Have you ever had things going great but then suddenly you hear the waterfall coming? It is terrifying to see the end of your world coming at you and there is no way to get out of this boat.

Oddly enough, this is the way God usually brings promotion. What looks like the end of your world, is actually the beginning of a new era. The way up in the kingdom, is down. The greatest among you, will be your servant. Going over the cliff, is actually going up. Still it looks terrifying when it is coming at you and things will look better when you have gone through it.

If you hear the waterfall approaching, brace yourself for the ride of your life, but remember: this will work out for your good. To go to a new level you must go over this waterfall.

Prayer: *Heavenly Father, I know that this will work out for my good. You will get me through this and I will come out a better person, in the name of Jesus I pray.*

Bible Fun Fact: The first people to ever see a rainbow were Noah and his sons. (Genesis 9:8, 13).

Day 32

† Poetic Justice †

*For Haman son of Hammedatha, the Agagite, the enemy of all the Jews, had plotted against the Jews to destroy them and had cast the pur (that is, the lot) for their ruin and destruction. But when the plot came to the king's attention, he issued written orders that the evil scheme Haman had devised against the Jews should come back onto his own head, and that he and his sons should be impaled on poles. **Esther 9:23–25 NIV***

It was a perfect day, Haman thought. He had just been invited to a feast that Queen Esther had prepared for the king and him. That pest that disrespected him at the city gate, Mordecai, would be hanged today, and all of his people would soon be annihilated as well. That should teach them to show some respect.

After showing up at the banquet though, that is where things started to go wrong for Haman. It turned out that Mordecai had raised the Queen as his own daughter. Overnight, the plan that Haman had made for God's people, came on himself. He and his sons were hanged and Mordecai took his place in leadership.

Nothing that anyone devises against you will work in the long term. God can cause the most elaborate of plans to fall back on the ones that started it. Keep your head up, do not get distracted and fall to their level. When God takes care of it, it is truly poetic justice.

Prayer: *Heavenly Father, I know that You are working in my life and I give You permission to do whatever You need to. In the end, this is going to work out for my good and I choose to trust You, in the name of Jesus I pray.*

Bible Fun Fact: Only Joseph is said to have been placed in a "coffin" (Gen 50:26).

Day 33

† The Roller Coaster †

After many days the word of the LORD came to Elijah, in the third year, saying, "Go, show yourself to Ahab, and I will send rain upon the earth."
1Kings 18:1 ESV

I remember some friends once got me on a roller coaster. We waited for everyone to board and then it started slowly climbing up and up the rails. After a pretty long wait, it crossed the crest of the hill and the real ride began. It was pretty boring until it started and then oh my…hang on!

Elijah waited for three years, just waiting, waiting, and then waiting some more. But when the Lord spoke this scripture to him, within hours, he had a showdown with 950 false prophets, caused fire to come down from heaven, executed the false prophets, turned Israel back to the Lord, caused it to rain when it had not for three years, and then outran a chariot back to town. I think he had crossed the top of the hill and was hanging on for dear life at that point.

Don't give up on God during the hill climb. When His

plan finally comes together it can move very quickly and you can be racing just to stay up with Him. The roller coaster climbs the hill slowly but when God says it is now time, hang on for the ride to come.

Prayer: *Heavenly Father, thank You for being there for me. Though it comes slow, I know that it is coming and that You have plans for me. Guide me and teach me along the way, in the name of Jesus I pray.*

Bible Fun Fact: What animal provided tax money for Jesus: A Fish!

Day 34

† Something From Nothing †

However, not to give offense to them, go to the sea and cast a hook and take the first fish that comes up, and when you open its mouth you will find a shekel. Take that and give it to them for me and for yourself. **Matt 17:27 ESV**

When Jesus came to Capernaum, the tax collectors asked Peter for taxes. Jesus told him to go fishing and the first fish that he caught would have a silver coin in its mouth, and to use that to pay them. What are the chances of that? I grew up fishing and never caught one like that.

Once when out of work for a season, I really needed two-hundred-fifty dollars to pay a bill and had no way to get it. After I went to church that Sunday, I noticed an envelope tucked into my Bible. When I opened it, there were two one-hundred dollar bills and a fifty. I still do not know for sure who did it, but they certainly heard from the Lord that time.

We like to be self sustaining, and to have to depend on others is a struggle. But when you find that you have to depend on God, you will find that He is more than enough.

So today if you find yourself in a tight spot, know that He is able to help you. Don't give up. God Almighty is the one that brings something, from nothing.

Prayer: *Heavenly Father, You know my needs before I even ask, and You know the things that I am facing. Please provide for me and boost my faith along the way, in the name of Jesus I pray.*

Bible Fun Fact: *As a sign to Hezekiah, God caused the sun's shadow on a sundial to go back ten degrees (Isa 38:7-8).*

Day 35

† The Last Minute †

He waited seven days, the time appointed by Samuel. But Samuel did not come to Gilgal, and the people were scattering from him. So Saul said, "Bring the burnt offering here to me, and the peace offerings." And he offered the burnt offering. As soon as he had finished offering the burnt offering, behold, Samuel came. **1 Samuel 13:8–10 ESV**

Samuel had told Saul to meet him at Gilgal and that he would make an offering and tell Saul what he must do in the coming battle. Saul waited the seven days but when his army started to scatter, he panicked and made the offering himself. Of course, as soon as Saul finished his offering Samuel showed up.

When the deadline starts approaching we often start sweating, panicking, what are we going to do? Where is God? They say God is never late but He also is not early. He arrives right on time. We are the ones that start to waver, and it is usually right before God shows up.

Do not give up yet. God's help and provision for you is closer than ever. Often we find that when we reach the end of our rope, that God is there to catch us. To us, it seems like the very last minute.

Prayer: *Heavenly Father, I pray that You help me to hang on, draw me to You and give me a clear vision. Change my heart and cause me to trust in You, in the name of Jesus I pray.*

Bible Fun Fact: A man had a bed 13 1/2 feet long and 6 feet wide. (Deuteronomy 3:11).

Day 36

† Rags To Riches †

Then the king gave Daniel high honors and many great gifts, and made him ruler over the whole province of Babylon and chief prefect over all the wise men of Babylon. **Dan. 2:48 ESV**

Daniel, who was born of royal family, was taken prisoner when Nebuchadnezzar captured Jerusalem in 597 BC. He was taken from his homeland, made a eunuch and a servant in Babylon against his will. It wasn't the happiest of starts, but in due time, God raised him up to second-in-command and he was the wisest man in Babylon.

Joseph was born his father's favorite, but then sold into slavery, served time in prison, and then was promoted to second-in-command to Pharaoh. Moses was raised and educated as Pharaoh's royal family, then spent forty years tending sheep in the wilderness, but became the most powerful man living on earth. David was anointed by Samuel and then ran from Saul for years before he actually became the king.

God has a plan for you. Before it comes to pass

though, there is a time of proving, pruning, and maturing. To us, it often looks like just plain waiting. Do not get discouraged while you are in the wilderness. God is completely faithful and the things that He has spoken to you, He will bring to pass. You cannot have a rags to riches story without the rags.

Prayer: *Heavenly Father, I wait on You. I thank You so much for all that You are doing in my life and I know that You will guide me down the best possible path. Have Your way in my life, in the name of Jesus I pray.*

Bible Fun Fact: *The longest verse in the Old Testament: (Esther 8:9).*

Day 37

† I Want To Hold Your Hand †

Whenever Moses held up his hand, Israel prevailed, and whenever he lowered his hand, Amalek prevailed. But Moses' hands grew weary, so they took a stone and put it under him, and he sat on it, while Aaron and Hur held up his hands, one on one side, and the other on the other side. So his hands were steady until the going down of the sun. And Joshua overwhelmed Amalek and his people with the sword. **Ex. 17:11-13 ESV**

When things are going well in your life it is easy to pray, even though we may neglect to. But when things get so badly that you go into survival mode, you need others to pray for you. There are times when you cannot walk alone, and it is you that is standing in the need of prayer.

I have seen times when more than anything, I needed to pray but no longer had the words, the energy, the faith, the willpower, or the hope to pray any longer. Exhausted, I sank into dark despair, but my church friends prayed for me constantly, and things in my life began to change. Their prayers for me were answered.

Today, if you are walking alone while your world is crumbling around you, share it with believers and get them to pray with you. It works. If you have no one like that, then you need to find believers that will. Start by visiting the nearest church and meeting with the pastor. If you cannot do that then send us your prayer request. Even if your life is great, be sure that you walk with other believers that will stand with you in the bad times. In this life, you sometimes need others to hold your hand.

Prayer: *Heavenly Father, I pray that You put the people in my life that should be there. Separate me from bad influences and replace them with good ones. Stir my heart to pray for those around me and raise up those that will pray for me, in the name of Jesus I pray.*

Bible Fun Fact: God caused the sun to stand still in the sky for 24 hours straight (Joshua 10:12-14).

Day 38

† The Pen And The Crackers †

Therefore do not be anxious, saying, What shall we eat? or What shall we drink? or What shall we wear? For the Gentiles seek after all these things, and your heavenly Father knows that you need them all. But seek first the kingdom of God and His righteousness, and all these things will be added to you. **Matthew 6:31–33 ESV**

One of the sweetest testimonies that I ever heard was from a missionary visiting our church. While on a plane heading to the mission field, she dug through her purse trying to find a pen to make notes with, but she could not find one. Also she was hungry because she had not eaten before the flight, and they did not serve food on the plane. She normally carried a pack of crackers for such a time but had none with her.

The missionary had brought along one Bible to give away, and when the plane landed, she started looking for a native to give it to. Finally she found a woman that she could communicate with and offered her the bible. The woman burst into tears and explained that she had been praying for a Bible for one whole year. The woman then reached into her purse for money but explained that she only had a pen, and a pack of crackers which she handed to the missionary.

If it matters to you, it matters to God. The small things in your life that you would not pray about, He knows about. When we get wrapped up in ourselves, we miss so much of what He has to offer. Place the Lord at the center of your life and these things will automatically happen. He has the pen and the crackers waiting.

Prayer: *Heavenly Father, I seek Your face and a deeper relationship with You today. I know that You will take care of my needs and fulfill the desires of my heart. Lord I put You first, in the name of Jesus I pray.*

Day 39

† Half-Starved Lions †

Then the king was exceedingly glad, and commanded that Daniel be taken up out of the den. So Daniel was taken up out of the den, and no kind of harm was found on him, because he had trusted in his God. **Daniel 6:23 ESV**

They took Daniel to the edge of the lions' den and let him see all of the half-starved lions prowling below them. The stench drifting upwards was horrible. I am sure the soldiers stood back a little ways as they pushed him to the edge of the pit. Then with a shove Daniel was falling through the air, right into the hungry mouths below.

On the way down he could hardly believe that after serving God and the kings uncompromisingly for over eighty years, that he was now being fed to the lions. What a retirement plan this was…they sealed the pit with a stone and it became dark with the sound of panting hungry lions pacing the floor. After a long dark stress-filled night, the dawn finally came and Daniel was unharmed. He was taken out of the pit, and his enemies were thrown in and devoured.

Tomorrow will be a better day. The dawn will come and no matter how bad it looks at night you will come through it unscathed. God will deliver you from the half-starved lions. As Daniel did in his darkest hour, just continue to trust in God.

Prayer: *Heavenly Father, I ask that You deliver me from the enemy. Protect me and my family Lord. Right the wrongs in my life and give me a fresh vision for the future, in the name of Jesus I pray.*

Bible Fun Fact: A parable is a short story that was told by Jesus. They were earthly stories with heavenly meanings.

Day 40

† Slow Train Coming †

Then Pharaoh sent and called Joseph, and they quickly brought him out of the pit. And when he had shaved himself and changed his clothes, he came in before Pharaoh. **Genesis 41:14 ESV**

Joseph had been in prison for over two years, and had been sold as a slave by his brothers years before that. Now he was standing before the pharaoh of Egypt and being given his signet ring. Suddenly, he was the second-in-command of the most powerful nation on earth. Prison in the morning, Ruler of Egypt in the evening. His dream had seemed to take forever, but it had now arrived.

This day was part of God's plan for Joseph and had taken between thirteen to twenty years to come to pass. It was intricate in detail and there were many layers and characters involved in making this happen. Israel was saved during an intense famine. Joseph learned management skills. He was humbled and became a broken man that God could use. There was over a decade of Joseph feeling forgotten, but suddenly his dream came to pass.

God's plans are intricate, deep, and all the pieces have to line up. This can take time, but suddenly it will happen, and it will happen. Keep on doing what you are supposed to do. Don't neglect your part of the plan and be sure to work with Him. God's plan for you may take time, but it will arrive right on schedule.

Prayer: *Heavenly Father, I pray that You stir me, wake me, give me a fresh fire and cause me to live Your perfect plan for my life. Move the things that need to be moved and open the doors that need to be opened. In the name of Jesus I pray.*

If there is any advice that I could give you, it would be this:

- There is an Almighty God. You are not Him so lighten up and don't try to be.
- When you fall, repent and get up, it is not over. God is always interested in your future.
- Take it one day at a time. Do not get too happy at success, or too sad at failure.
- God wants a relationship with you, more than you do with Him.
- God is never mean.
- God's love is unconditional, but His blessings are not. Give and it will be given to you. Honor your father and mother and your days will be prolonged…there is a pattern here.
- The way up, is down. The more humility there is in your life, the further God can take you. Moses was the meekest man on earth.
- Get to know the Holy Spirit.

Dion Todd

Thank you so much for reading!

We hope that you have enjoyed reading this devotional. You can find more of our writing at www.diontodd.org. Have a blessed day and I pray that the Lord works His perfect will in your life. May He guide you into the path that He has laid out and cause you to have all that you have need of, in the name of Jesus.

If you have never asked the Lord Jesus into your life and want to experience a relationship with Him, then pray this to get started:

Lord Jesus, please forgive me and come into my life. Be my Lord and Savior. Guide me from this day forth and fill me with Your Holy Spirit. I surrender to You today.

36762113R00055

Made in the USA
Charleston, SC
18 December 2014